More Old Git Wit

summersdale

MORE OLD GIT WIT

Copyright © Summersdale Publishers Ltd, 2008
This selection was compiled by Aubrey Malone.

Illustrations by Ian Baker.

Summersdale Publishers Ltd
46 West Street
Chichester
West Sussex
PO19 1RP
UK

www.summersdale.com

Printed and bound in Great Britain

ISBN: 978-1-84024-692-6

Disclaimer
Every effort has been made to attribute the quotations in this collection to the correct source. Should there be any omissions or errors in this respect we apologise and shall be pleased to make the appropriate acknowledgements in any future editions.

More Old Git Wit

Aubrey Malone

Contents

Editor's Note

Whether you're desperate to cling onto your youth or keen to join the ranks of the 'older and wiser' generation, getting old is one of life's inevitabilities.

As time ticks by we are all forced to accept a waistline expanding more quickly than our granny pants can keep up with, frequent visits to the doctor's surgery and an inexplicable urge to sport a blue rinse.

Despite the reading glasses, hearing aids and false teeth of these veterans, their sarcastic comments and witty remarks show that at least their sense of humour has remained firmly in place – even if everything else has taken a somewhat saggy journey southwards.

Delight in the glory of the good old days and laugh out loud at bizarre epitaphs and obituaries as age-afflicted academics, comedians and actors share the trials and tribulations of getting old – some more disgracefully than others!

Prescribe yourself a hearty dose of light-hearted humour with this selection of quotes, one-liners and witticisms from oldies who really should know better. It's just what the doctor ordered.

AMBITIONS

God grant me the
senility to forget the
people I never liked.

Terry Wogan

He said he planned to live for 200 years. I replied, 'Good, I'll be one of your pall-bearers.'

Angelo Fusco

I'd hate to die with a good liver, good kidneys and a good brain. When I die I want everything to be knackered.

Hamish Imlach

When I die I want to be
buried in the 'No Smoking'
section of the graveyard.

Spike Milligan

I'm aiming to stop being an
adolescent by the time I'm 50.

Wendy Cage

I want to live to be 80 so I
can piss more people off.

Charles Bukowski

What I look forward
to is continued
immaturity, followed
by death.

Dave Barry

I wouldn't like to die on stage.
I'd settle for room service and a
couple of dissipated women.

Peter O'Toole

When I die I want to be cremated,
and ten per cent of my ashes
thrown in my agent's face.

W. C. Fields

I should like to die in Manchester.
The transition between
Manchester and death would
be almost unnoticeable.

Lord Roseberry

When I die I want to go like my
grandfather, peacefully in his sleep.
Not screaming, like his passengers.

Anonymous

When I die I want to leave my
body to science fiction.

Steven Wright

AGEING ROUND THE MIDDLE

Middle age is when you're willing to give up your seat to a lady on the bus, and can't.

Sammy Kaye

Middle age is the period in
life when your idea of getting
ahead is staying even.

Herbert Prochnow

One of the hardest decisions in
life is when to start middle age.

Clive James

Beware of what you wish for
in youth, for in middle age
you will surely achieve it.

Johann W. Von Goethe

Youth tends to look
ahead. Old age
tends to look back.
Middle age tends
to look worried.

James Simpson

I wouldn't mind being called
middle-aged if I knew a few
more 100-year-old people.

Dean Martin

Middle age is when we can do just as
much as ever – but would rather not.

Dan Kiely

You know you've reached middle
age when the kids will allow you
to pick them up from school,
but not get out of the car.

Gary Ryan

The hands of my biological
clock are giving me the fingers.

Wendy Liebman

Middle age is when you look at
the rain teeming down and say,
'That'll be good for the garden.'

Grace Marshall

Women stop worrying about
becoming pregnant and men start
worrying about looking like they are.

Fred Metcalf on middle age

Middle age is the time of life that
a man first notices in his wife.

Richard Armour

BEING A
GRANDPARENT

My grandmother's
90. She's dating.
He's 93. They never
argue. They can't
hear each other.

Cathy Ladman

My grandfather reached a
hundred and was then shot
by a jealous husband.

Finlay Currie

My grandmother is 92 years
old and she hasn't a single
grey hair. She's bald.

Bernard Manning

Granny said she was going to grow
old gracefully, but she left it too late.

Christine Kelly

24

It's great being a grandmother.
You can send the kids home.

Whoopi Goldberg

When my husband left... he
said, 'I don't mind being a
grandfather, but I don't want to
be married to a grandmother.'

Viveca Lindfors

Anytime I appear on television my granny turns her hearing aid off.

Julian Clary

What's the difference between an Italian grandmother and an elephant? Twenty pounds and a black dress.

Jim Davidson

Grandma would always take the news of a death hard with a gasp of, 'My God, I don't have a thing to wear.'

Erma Bombeck

My grandfather told me too much sex would make me go blind. He had his glasses on at the time.

Bill Hicks

MEMORY'S THE FIRST THING TO GO

I remember your name
perfectly. I just can't
think of your face.

Oscar Wilde

Whenever I meet a man whose name I can't remember, I give myself two minutes. If it is a hopeless case, I always say 'And how is the old complaint?'

Charles Dickens

My grandfather found a cure for amnesia, but he could never remember what it was.

Henny Youngman

It's OK to have sex after a heart attack. But don't forget to close the ambulance door.

Phyllis Diller

How comforting it is, once or twice a year, to get together and forget the old times.

James Fenton

A woman never forgets her age
– once she decides what it is.

Stanley Davis

The older we get, the
better we used to be.

John McEnroe

31

God gave us our memories so that
we might have roses in December.

J. M. Barrie

Do you remember the good old
days? And the bad old nights?

Bob Monkhouse

I have a memory like an elephant. In fact elephants often consult me.

Nöel Coward

By the time you reach 75 years of age you've learnt everything. All you have to do is try and remember it.

George Coote

Remembering
something at the
first try is now as
good as an orgasm.

Gloria Steinem

ROMANTIC YEARNINGS

I used to demand
good looks. Now
all I ask for is a
healthy prostate.

Joan Rivers

My husband will never chase
another woman. He's too
fine, too decent... too old.

Gracie Allen

———

Bill Wyman couldn't be here
tonight. He's at the hospital
attending the birth of his next wife.

Frank Worthington

———

You can both be in nappies
at the same time.

Sue Kolinsky on the advantage
of having children at 60

An old man marrying a young
girl is like buying a book for
someone else to read.

Jim Thompson

———— • ————

He gave her a 20-carat diamond
and she gave him the mumps.

Stanley Davis on a millionaire and his child bride

———— • ————

I asked the life insurance man what
I'd get if my husband died tomorrow,
'About fifteen years,' he told me.

Bette Davis

A man of 90 married a woman of 85. They spent the honeymoon trying to get out of the car.

Hal Roach

The widower married his first wife's sister so he wouldn't have to break in a new mother-in-law.

Tony Hancock

I must be getting old. I can't take yes for an answer.

Fred Allen

Wives are young men's mistresses,
companions for middle age,
and old men's nurses.

Francis Bacon

———•———

Marriage is a wonderful
institution, but who wants
to live in an institution?

Groucho Marx

———•———

I'm all for May–December
romances, but BC and AD?

Michael Harkness on the marriage of Michael
Douglas and Catherine Zeta-Jones

My best chat-up line? 'Hi,
I'm Hugh Hefner.'

Hugh Hefner at 72

———

Here's God's cruel joke: by
the time a guy figures out how
women work, his penis doesn't.

Adam Carolla

———

Old? He chases his
secretary around the desk
but can't remember why.

Leopold Fechtner

When you're 60 you get
social security, not girls.

Neil Simon

—◆—

My wife told me I'd drive
her to the grave. I had the
car out in two minutes.

Tommy Cooper

—◆—

Yes, I'm dating again but I
can't say any more. We don't
want to rush into anything.

George Burns at 93

Liz Taylor has been married so many
times she has rice marks on her face.

Don Rickles

The old theory was, 'Marry an
older man because they're more
mature.' The new one is, 'Men don't
mature. Marry a younger one.'

Rita Rudner

BODILY BETRAYAL

My body, on the
move, resembles
in sight and sound
nothing so much
as a bin liner full
of yoghurt.

Stephen Fry

When I hit my thirties I found
there was less hair on my
head and more in my ears.

Robert Wuhl

I try to wear my scarf so tightly
fixed under my chin that it holds
in place the loose flesh.

Quentin Crisp

I've started to use my left
breast as a bath plug.

Joan Rivers

They say you're only as old
as you feel; in which case I
probably died six years ago.

Joe O'Connor

She couldn't wait to be old
enough to get a facelift so
she could look younger.

Gene Perret

It is obscene to think that
some day one will look like
an old map of France.

Brigitte Bardot

I'm so old that when I get
up in the morning I sound
like I'm making popcorn.

Lawrence Taylor

Jo Brand's facelift didn't work. They found another one just like it underneath.

Garry Bushell

———•———

Old cooks never die. They just go to pot.

Nigel Rees

I've spent so much money on
plastic surgery it would have been
cheaper to change my DNA.

Joan Rivers

❧

The best way to prevent sagging
as you grow older is to keep
eating till the wrinkles fall out.

John Candy

A lot of girls would have
hourglass figures if time
hadn't shifted the sands.

Stanley Davis

I'm ageing about as well as
a beach party movie.

Harvey Fierstein

Old age puts more wrinkles in
our minds than on our faces.

Michel de Montaigne

— • —

I have a body like a rebuilt jeep.

Ernest Hemingway

— • —

I'm in pretty good shape
for the shape I'm in.

Mickey Rooney at 58

I'm so wrinkled I can screw my hat on.

Phyllis Diller

———•———

I don't want anything else on
my body that might fall off.

Gene Perret on refusing to wear a beeper

———•———

Drinking removes warts and
wrinkles from women I look at.

Jackie Gleason

Old age is when things begin to
wear out, fall out and spread out.

Beryl Pfizer

Old accountants never die.
They just lose their figures.

Audrey Austin

An incurable optimist is a bloke
who gets married at 88 and
buys a house near a school.

Frank Carson

COMPENSATIONS

No one expects
you to run into a
burning building.

Sonya Plowman on the benefits of being old

When people are old enough
to know better, they're old
enough to do worse.

Hesketh Pearson

If you live long enough the
venerability factor creeps in. You get
accused of things you never did, and
praised for virtues you never had.

Laurence J. Peter

Death is one of the few
things that can be done just
as easily standing up.

Woody Allen

———◆———

Being 80 makes me feel
like an authority, especially
when I say, 'I don't know.'

Peter Ustinov

They told me if I got older
I'd get wiser. In that case I
must now be a genius.

George Burns

Getting old is a bit like being drunk.
Everyone else looks brilliant.

Billy Connolly

The great comfort of turning
40 is the realisation that you
are now too old to die young.

Paul Dickson

One of the many pleasures
of age is looking back at the
people one didn't marry.

Rodney Dangerfield

THE SECRETS OF
STAYING YOUNG

On her 107th birthday
she attributed her
great age to the
fact that she'd never
had a boyfriend.

The Star

Whenever anyone asks myself
and my wife if we have any children
I say, 'Yes, one boy aged 44.'

Tony Hancock… at 44

—·—

Why have I lived so long?
Jack Daniels and not taking
shit from the press.

Frank Sinatra

—·—

My parents have been married for 55
years. The secret to their longevity?
Outlasting your opponent.

Cathy Ladman

He was either a man of 150 who
was rather young for his years,
or a man of about 110 who
had been aged by trouble.

P.G. Wodehouse

A very old twelve.

Nöel Coward after being asked what age
a woman looked after a facelift.

People say I'm into my second
childhood. The reality is that
I never left my first one.

Spike Milligan

Good cheekbones
are the brassiere
of old age.

Barbara de Portago

REGRETS, I'VE HAD A FEW

The only thing that bothers me about growing older is that when I see a pretty girl now it arouses my memory instead of my hopes.

Milton Berle

One starts to get young at the age of 60, and then it is too late.

Pablo Picasso

———•———

I often sit back and think, 'I wish I'd done that'... and find out that I already have.

Richard Harris

Oh to be 70 again!

Georges Clemenceau on his 80th
birthday after spotting a pretty girl

Any regrets? Yes, I'd like to
have tried more positions.

Groucho Marx at 72

Nostalgia ain't what it used to be.

Jackie Mason

———•———

If I had my life to live over, I'd like to live over a Chinese restaurant.

John Junkin

———•———

My only regret in life is that I didn't drink more champagne.

John Maynard Keynes

I have more skeletons
in my closet than the
Smithsonian Institute.

Ben Jones

Early to rise and early to bed makes
a man healthy, wealthy and dead.

James Thurber

Old age is the happiest time
in a man's life. The worst of
it is, there's so little of it.

W. S. Gilbert

I wasted time, and now
doth time waste me.

William Shakespeare, *Richard III*

DOCTOR, I'M IN TROUBLE

My husband hasn't been a well man, I've had his prostate hanging over my head for years.

Dame Edna Everage

There is no human activity
which some doctor somewhere
won't discover leads directly
to cardiac arrest.

John Mortimer

❖

You die of a heart attack with
the Atkins diet, but so what?
At least you die thin.

Bob Geldof

❖

Too late for fruit, too
soon for flowers.

Walter de La Mare after recovering
from a life-threatening illness

When I was admitted to the heart unit, somebody sent me a 'Get Well' card that said, 'We didn't know you had one.'

Brian Clough

The best part of a hospital is the exit door.

Tom Brady

73

My doctor told me I
had hypochondria. 'Not
that as well!' I said.

Kenny Everett

The doctor told me I was in
good shape for a man of 70.
It's a pity I'm only 50.

Les Dawson

The doctor told his patient he
had Alzheimer's and cancer.
The patient replied, 'Oh well,
at least I don't have cancer.'

Henny Youngman

I don't want to put my life
in the hands of anyone who
believes in reincarnation.

Glenn Super on Indian doctors

My doctor told me
to watch my drinking,
so now I do it in
front of the mirror.

Rodney Dangerfield

Doctors are always telling us that drinking shortens your life. Well I've seen more old drunkards than old doctors.

Edward Phillips

A miracle drug is any one that will do what the label says.

Eric Hodgins

I had a cholesterol test. They found bacon.

Bob Zany

'Doctor, my irregular
heartbeat is bothering me.'
'Don't worry, we'll soon
put a stop to that.'

Fred Metcalf

***

My doctor said I looked like a million
dollars – all green and wrinkled.

Red Skelton

***

I went to the doctor. 'How do
I stand?' I asked him. He said,
'It's a bloody mystery to me.'

Les Dawson

My doctor told me to do something
that puts me out of breath, so
I've taken up smoking again.

Jo Brand

My doctor told me to do something

The ultimate indignity is to be
given a bedpan by a stranger who
calls you by your first name.

Maggie Kuhn

My doctor gave me three pills.
The blue one is for before dinner.
The red one is for after dinner,
and the yellow one is dinner.

Leopold Fechtner

I'm a bit worried about my last
visit to the doctor. He told me
not to start reading any serials.

Danny Cummings

EXERCISE

My best exercise
these days is rolling my
oxygen tank around
like a beach ball when
I get out of bed.

Marlon Brando

The only exercise I get these days
is taking the cufflinks out of one
shirt and putting them into another.

Ring Lardner

❖

I'm pushing 60. That's
enough exercise for me.

Mark Twain

❖

Do I exercise? Well I once
jogged to the ashtray.

Will Self

If you want to know
what you'll look like in
ten years' time, look
in the mirror after
you've run a marathon.

Jeff Scaff

The only form of exercise
I take is massage.

Truman Capote

I had a muscle that twitched all
day yesterday. It's the most
exercise I've had in years.

Terry Martin

BIRTHDAYS

I'm pleading with my
wife to have birthdays
again. I don't want
to grow old alone.

Rodney Dangerfield

I'm not like Jane Fonda or any of
those other women who say how
fabulous they think it is to turn
40. I think it's a crock of shit.

Cher

Birthdays are nature's way of
telling us to eat more cake.

Jo Brand

The only time a woman wishes
she were a year older is when
she's having a baby.

Mary Marsh

My wife said to me, 'I don't look 50, do I darling?' I said, 'Not any more.'

Bob Monkhouse

Zsa Zsa Gabor has just celebrated the 41st anniversary of her 39th birthday.

Joan Rivers

Pushing 40? She's clinging onto it for dear life.

Ivy Compton-Burnett

By the time I lit the last candle
on my birthday cake, the
first one had gone out.

George Burns at 80

He had too many birthdays.

Andy Marx explaining the cause of his
father Groucho's death in 1977

I tried to count the candles on my birthday cake...the heat kept driving me back.

Bob Hope

Birthdays only come once a year unless you're Joan Collins, in which case they only come every four years.

Steven Bauer

Eighty is the time of
your life when even
your birthday suit
needs pressing

Bob Hope

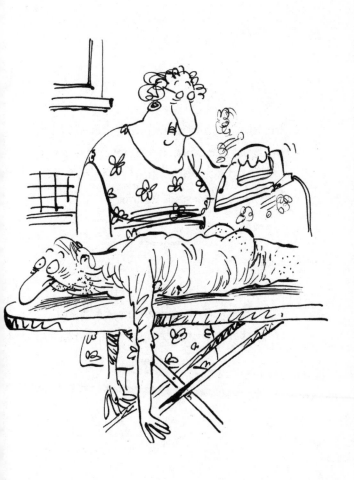

One day I said to myself, 'I'm 40.' By the time I recovered from the shock of that discovery I had reached 50.

Simone de Beauvoir

Passing your 80th birthday is a wonderful achievement. You just sit there and it happens.

Angus McBean

RETIREMENT

When you're not
interested in trying
new things, that's
when you should start
hitting golf balls.

Clint Eastwood

Americans hardly ever retire from business. They're either carried out feet first or they jump from a window.

A. L. Goodhart

I want to retire at 50. I want to play cricket and geriatric football and sing in the choir.

Neil Kinnock

It's too late for me to retire now.

Michael Caine at 70

I'm retired, but it's an Irish retirement
so I have to work to support it.

Dave Allen

—•—

I wasn't very flattered by the boss
on my retirement day. He said he
wasn't so much losing a worker
as gaining a parking space.

Fred Allen

—•—

Lady Bancroft and I have 80,000
golden reasons for retiring, and every
one of them is lodged in the bank.

Squire Bancroft

You don't need to retire as an actor. There are lots of parts you can play lying in bed and in wheelchairs.

Judi Dench

———

An insurance salesman just signed me up for a marvellous retirement policy. If I keep up the payments for ten years, he can retire.

Fred Metcalf

YOU KNOW YOU'RE GETTING OLD WHEN...

You know you're getting old when the girl you smile at thinks you're one of her father's friends.

Alan Murray

You know you're getting old when
you get winded playing cards.

George Burns

❦

You know you're getting older when
the policemen start looking younger.

Arnold Bennett

❦

You're getting old when the
gleam in your eyes is from the
sun hitting your bifocals.

Herbert Prochnow

You know you're getting old when
you go back to your class reunion
and they serve prune punch.

Chi Chi Rodriguez

❧

When he first started going to
school, history wasn't even a subject.

Mort Sahl on Bob Hope

❧

You know you're getting old
when your 'get up and go'
just got up and went.

Brendan Grace

You try and straighten out
the wrinkles in your socks and
discover you're not wearing any.

Leonard Knott

You know you're getting old when
people tell you how well you look.

Alan King

SENIOR SEX

It's sex, not youth, that's wasted on the young.

Janet Harris

In my thirties I was doing it. In my forties I was organising it. Now, unfortunately, I can only talk about it.

Former brothel madam Cynthia Payne in 2004

❦

My best contraceptive these days is taking my clothes off in front of my husband.

Phyllis Diller

❦

Everything that goes up must come down. But there comes a time when not everything that's down can come up.

George Burns

When you get older your body changes. Now I groan louder after a meal than I do after an orgasm.

Joel Warshaw

❧

Her husband didn't hold anything against her. He was too old.

Jim Davidson

❧

So Rod Stewart got married again. Where's he going on honeymoon – Viagra Falls?

Gordon McDonald

Why do we talk about
dirty old men, but
never dirty old women?

Dave Allen

Virility at 21 is considered
lechery at 71.

Dr George Giarchi

❧—✦—☙

Are there sexy dead ones?

Sean Connery after being informed he was
voted 'The Sexiest Man Alive' in a poll.

❧—✦—☙

Sex in the sixties is great,
but improves if you pull over
to the side of the road.

Johnny Carson

CREATIVE
MATHEMATICS

I've told so many lies
about my age I've
made my children
illegitimate.

Jessie Kesson

I would say I was 99, dahling.

Zsa Zsa Gabor after being asked what she would do if she lived to be 100

—◆—

If you're 39, tell people you're 55 and they'll think you look brilliant.

Frank Hall

—◆—

Candidates must be over 35, and where are you going to find a woman who'll admit to that?

Bob Hope on why a woman could never be President of America

Allow me to put the record straight: I am 46, and have been for some years past.

Erica Jong

———

Thirty-five is a very attractive age for a woman. London society is full of women who have remained 35 for years.

Oscar Wilde

———

The worst thing anybody ever said to me is that I'm 60. Which I am.

Joan Rivers

Looking 50 is great,
especially if you're 60.

Fran Lebowitz

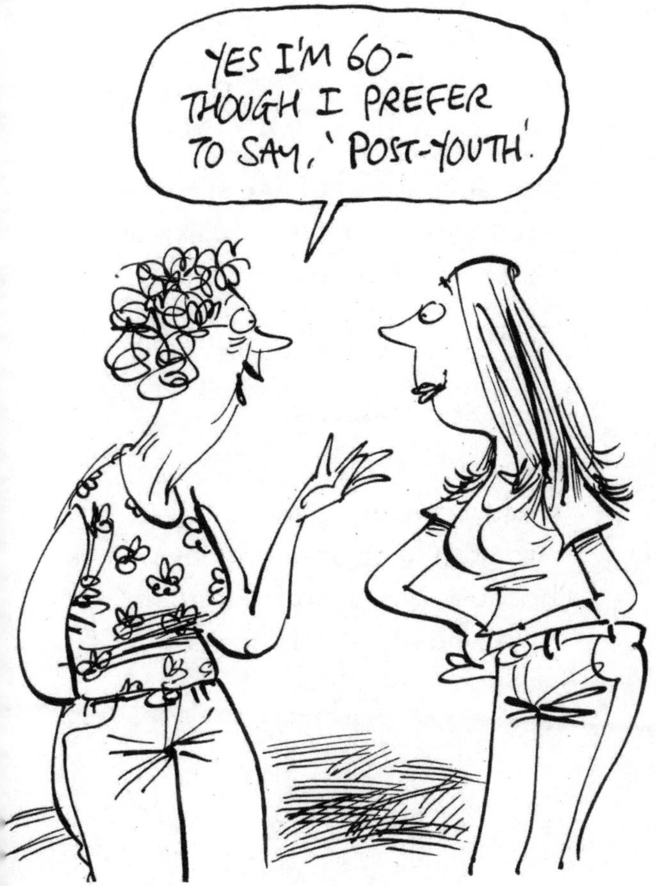
YES I'M 60- THOUGH I PREFER TO SAY, 'POST-YOUTH'.

She asked me what age she was...
'I'm not sure,' I said eventually, 'but
whatever it is, you don't look it.'

Sid Caesar

❦

My mother is going to have
to stop lying about her age
because pretty soon I'm going
to be older than she is.

Tripp Evans

The best years of Joan
Collins' life were the ten
years between 39 and 40.

Don Rickles

———◆———

I just tell people I'm as old as my
wife. Then I lie about her age.

Fred Metcalf

———◆———

She said she was approaching
40, and I couldn't help wondering
from what direction.

Bob Hope

ADVICE

If you resolve to give up smoking, drinking and loving, you don't actually live longer. It just seems longer.

Clement Freud

Never put off until tomorrow
what you can do the day after.

Louis Safian

—•—

A woman should never give
birth after 35. Thirty-five is
enough kids for anyone.

Gracie Allen

—•—

I got on well by talking. Death could
not get a word in edgeways, grew
discouraged, and travelled on.

Louise Erdrich

I asked my doctor
what I should do after
having a pacemaker
put in. He said,
'Keep paying your
electricity bill.'

Roger Moore

Don't complain about growing old.
Many are denied the privilege.

Somerset Maugham

Avoid school reunions. The last man
I met who was at school with me had
a long white beard and no teeth.

P.G. Wodehouse

It's not how old you are,
it's how you're old.

Brian Blessed

The only thing for old age
is a brave face, a good tailor
and comfortable shoes.

Alan Ayckbourn

THE GOLDEN AGE
OF HOLLYWOOD

In Hollywood
sometimes you're dead
before you're dead.

Spencer Tracy

Nowadays when a fan runs up to me it's not to get my autograph but to have a better look at my wrinkles.

Liz Taylor

People say, 'Gosh, doesn't Teri Hatcher look amazing for 42?' Hello – I've got clothes older than that.

Joan Collins

When Marlene Dietrich
complained to her photographer
that he wasn't making her look
as beautiful as he used to, he
told her, 'I'm sorry Marlene, but
I'm seven years older now.'

Michael Harkness

An actress once said to Rosalind
Russell, 'I dread the thought of
45.' Russell looked at her and
said, 'Why – what happened?'

Steven Bauer

I haven't had a hit film since
Joan Collins was a virgin.

Burt Reynolds

I remember what someone of
60 looked like when I was a kid.
They didn't look like me.

Jack Nicholson

125

The only whistles I
get these days are
from the tea kettle.

Raquel Welch

Why do I never go to the Cannes
Film Festival? Because it's full
of people I hoped were dead.

Dirk Bogarde

❧

Catherine Zeta-Jones raised a few
eyebrows with her flirty behaviour
with actor Sean Connery, a man
old enough to be her husband.

Martin Clunes

❧

Joan Collins' career is a
testament to menopausal chic.

Erica Jong

Old Cary Grant Fine. How You?

Cary Grant replying to a telegram that
went, 'How Old Cary Grant?'

Old film directors never die
– they just fade to black.

Audrey Austin

I'm never quite sure whether I'm one
of the cinema's elder statesmen or
just the oldest whore on the beat.

Joseph L. Mankiewicz

TIME'S WINGED CHARIOT

At my back I often hear time's winged chariot changing gear.

Eric Linklater

George Burns is so old, he
has an autographed bible.

Sid Caesar

———•———

Bob Hope is alive, but only in the
sense that he can't be legally buried.

Steven Bauer

———•———

There comes a time in every
woman's life when the only thing
that helps is a glass of champagne.

Bette Davis

Inside every 70 year old is a 35 year
old asking, 'What happened?'

Ann Landers

An interviewer once asked me
how I felt getting up in the morning
at 88. 'Amazed,' I told him.

George Burns

Time is the best teacher.
Unfortunately, it kills all its students.

Billy Crystal

Life is a table d'hôte meal, with
Time changing the plates before
you've had enough of anything.

Tom Kettle

I don't know that my behaviour
has improved with age.

Jimmy Connors

FUNFERALLS

Funerals in Ireland are so jolly, they should be called funferalls.

James Joyce

Peter O'Toole looks like
he's walking around just to
save funeral expenses.

John Huston

I hate it at weddings when old
relatives tell me, 'You'll be next,
love.' I get my own back at funerals.

Mandy Knight

I refused to attend his funeral,
but I wrote a very nice letter
explaining that I approved of it.

Mark Twain

The reason so many people turned
up at Louis B. Mayer's funeral was
to make sure that he was dead.

Sam Goldwyn

———◆———

Movie actors wear dark glasses at
funerals to conceal the fact that
their eyes aren't red from weeping.

Nunally Jones

———◆———

Funerals are like bad movies.
They last too long, they're over-
acted, and the end is predictable.

George Burns

I dislike funerals so much I may
not even go to my own one.

Brian Behan

——•——

My father's funeral cost me ten
grand. I buried him in a rented suit.

Red Skelton

Is it worth our while
going home?

One old man to another at the funeral of a friend

I hope you die before me because I
don't want you singing at my funeral.

Spike Milligan to Harry Secombe

No matter how great a man is,
the size of his funeral usually
depends on the weather.

Rosemary Clooney

THE BRIGHT SIDE

Every day I beat my
own previous record
for the number of
consecutive days
I've stayed alive.

George Carlin

I woke up this morning and I was
still alive so I'm pretty cheerful.

Spike Milligan at 79

We are always the same age inside.

Gertrude Stein

Even if there's snow on the
roof, it doesn't mean the fire
has gone out in the furnace.

John Diefenbaker

I do not call myself old yet. Not till
a young woman offers me her seat
will that tragedy really be mine.

E. V. Lucas

To be 70 years young is sometimes
far more cheerful and hopeful
than to be 40 years old.

Oliver Wendell Holmes

Since I got to be 65, I look
better, feel better, make love
better and I never lied better.

George Burns

FROM HERE TO ETERNITY

Them that does all the talk about how nice it is in the next world, I don't see them in any great hurry to get there.

Brendan Behan

Death is all in the mind, really. Once
you're dead you forget all about it.

Jack Trevor-Storey

It's a funny old world. A man is
lucky to get out of it alive.

W. C. Fields

I believe in life after death, which
is strange, because at one time I
didn't believe in life after birth.

Ozzy Osbourne

If people really believe that
death leads to eternal bliss,
why do they wear seatbelts?

Doug Stanhope

147

For Catholics, death
is a promotion.

Bob Fosse

When men grow virtuous in their
old age, they only make a sacrifice
to God of the devil's leavings.

Alexander Pope

I think the resurrection of the
body, unless much improved in
construction, is a mistake.

Evelyn Underhill

The prospect of everlasting
life is vaguely disconcerting,
and you could end up sharing a
cloud with your bank manager.

Joe O'Connor

⬥

All men are cremated equal.

Ben Elton

⬥

I've had so many things done
to my body, when I die God
won't even recognise me.

Phyllis Diller

Death can be as simple as
falling off a log. Which is why
you should steer clear of logs.

Guy Browning

❧

My interest in the next life
is purely academic.

Brendan Behan

❧

If they don't have chocolate
in heaven I'm not going.

Roseanne Barr

Any man who has $10,000
left when he dies is a failure.

Errol Flynn

———•———

I don't want to go to heaven if
you have to stand all the time.

Spike Milligan

———•———

I don't think much of this one!

James Joyce's response when asked
what he thought of the next world

OH, BITCHERY

In obituaries, 'convivial' means drunk, 'a great raconteur' means crashing bore and 'relishing physical contact' describes a cruel sadist.

Vanora Bennett

I've just learned about his illness.
Let's hope it's nothing trivial.

Irvin S. Cobb

—•—

Age cannot wither him, nor
exhaust his infinite mendacity.

Tom Collins

—•—

Tonight we honour a man old
enough to be his own father.

Red Skelton introducing George Burns

Every morning I read the
obituary page over breakfast.
If I'm not in it, I get up.

Benjamin Franklin

⬥

They say you shouldn't say
nothing about the dead unless
it's good. He's dead. Good.

Jackie Mabley

AFFLICTIONS OF AGE

I don't deserve this.
But I have arthritis
and I don't deserve
that either.

Jack Benny on receiving an award
towards the end of his life

I used to play football when I was young but then my eyes went bad – so I became a referee.

Eric Morecambe

I do, and I hope to have it replaced very soon.

Terry Wogan on people saying he didn't know the meaning of 'hip'.

I've got to the stage where I need my
false teeth and my hearing aid before
I can ask where I've left my glasses.

Stuart Turner

I got used to my arthritis
To my dentures I'm resigned
I can manage my bifocals
But Lord I miss my mind.

Anon

The old have everything going for them. Their hair's going, their legs are going, their eyesight's going...

Denys Humphries

My knees are on their last legs.

Paul McGrath

Consciousness in my case is that annoying time between naps.

Bob Hope

When I get out of bed in the morning, the only thing that doesn't hurt is my pyjamas.

Terry Martin

'Do you know who I am?'
'No, but if you go up to the desk,
the matron might be able to help.'

Exchange between Gerald Ford and a patient at an
old folks home where he was making a speech

By the time a man is wise
enough to watch his step, he's
too old to go anywhere.

Earl Wilson

I have a problem about nearing 60. I keep waking up and thinking I'm 31.

Elizabeth Janeway

They say the first thing to go when you're old is your legs or your eyesight... The first thing to go is parallel parking.

Kurt Vonnegut

Old age means bringing a packed
lunch when you climb the stairs.

Paddy Murray

—◆—

The Alzheimer's patient's
favourite chat-up line is,
'Do I come here often?'

Terry Wogan

—◆—

It's not the hearing one misses,
but the overhearing.

David Wright

THE YOUNG

The denunciation
of the young greatly
assists the circulation
of the blood.

Logan Pearsall Smith

The old-fashioned respect for
the young is fast dying out.

Oscar Wilde

What is more enchanting than the
voices of young people when you
can't hear what they're saying?

Logan Pearsall Smith

Never raise your
hand to your children.
It leaves your mid-
section unprotected.

Robert Orben

Always pat children on the head
whenever you meet them, just in
case they happen to be yours.

Augustus John

— • —

Women who remember their first
kiss now have daughters who can't
remember their first husbands.

Henny Youngman

— • —

There are only two things a child
will share willingly: communicable
diseases and his mother's age.

Benjamin Spock

The trouble with the music
teenagers listen to these days
is that you can't tell when
the record is worn out.

Stanley Davis

———•———

The dead might as well try to speak
to the living as the old to the young.

Willa Cather

———•———

Youth is a disease from
which we all recover.

Dorothy Fuldheim

The young always have the same
problem – how to rebel and conform
at the same time. They have now
solved this by defying their parents
and copying one another.

Quentin Crisp

There's nothing wrong with
teenagers that reasoning with
them won't aggravate.

Jean Kerr

SOBERING THOUGHTS

The three ages of
man are under-age,
over-age and average.

Herbert Prochnow

Science has salvaged scrap
metal and even found vitamins
and valuable oils in refuse, but old
people are extravagantly wasted.

Anzia Yezierska

People ought to be either one
of two things: young or dead.

Dorothy Parker

For a while you're a veteran,
and then you're just old.

Lance Alworth

I'm very uncomfortable living in
a world where the Pope is 25
years younger than I am.

Billy Wilder in 1993

The living are the dead on holiday.

Maurice Maeterlinck

Old age is life's parody.

Simone De Beauvoir

I know I'm going to die
because my birth certificate
has an expiry date on it.

Steven Wright

There comes a time in every
man's life where he must make
way for an older man.

Reginald Maudling

WORDS AND MUSIC

A 'Selected Poems' anthology is like a clock awarded by an affable but faintly impatient employer.

Sean O'Brien

I dislike modern memoirs.
They're generally written by
people who have either lost their
memories or have never done
anything worth remembering.

Oscar Wilde

After a certain age, a poet's main
rival is the poet he used to be.

William Logan

You eventually reach an age
where every sentence bumps into
one you wrote 30 years ago.

John Updike

I was asked how we should
celebrate Harold Pinter's
fiftieth Birthday. I should have
suggested a minute's silence.

Alan Bennett

I'm old enough to remember Elvis
the first time he was alive.

Noel V. Ginnity

When I was young we didn't
have MTV. We had to take
drugs and go to concerts.

Steven Pearl

She was an ageing singer who had to take every note above 'A' with her eyebrows.

Montague Glass

I was a veteran before I was a teenager.

Michael Jackson

People tell me I'm
a legend. In other
words, a has-been.

Bob Dylan

The best epitaph for a blues
singer would be, 'Didn't
Wake Up This Morning'.

Burl Ives

People like their blues singers dead.

Janis Joplin

EXIT LINES:
FAMOUS LAST WORDS

Dear World, I am leaving because I am bored... Good luck.

Suicide note of George Sanders

Either that wallpaper goes or I do.

Oscar Wilde

No flowers please, just caviar.

Jennifer Paterson

Don't let it end like this. Tell them I said something.

Pancho Villa

Doctor, do you think it
could've been the sausage?

Paul Claudel

Keep Paddy behind the mixer.

Building tycoon Sir Alfred McAlpine

I told you I was ill.

Spike Milligan

Last Will and Testament: I, being of sound mind, have spent every penny.

Ray Ellington

❧

Quick – save the dessert.

Paulette Brillat-Savarin

❧

They couldn't hit an elephant at this dist-

General John Sedgwick

This is no time for making
new enemies.

Voltaire after a priest had asked him to
renounce the devil on his deathbed

Dear Elise, seek younger
friends. I am extinct.

George Bernard Shaw

I've just had 18 whiskies. I
think that's a record.

Dylan Thomas

Is there one who understands me?

James Joyce

All in all I'd prefer to be
in Philadelphia.

W. C. Fields

If this is dying, I don't think much of it.

Lytton Strachey

I should never have switched
from scotch to martinis.

Humphrey Bogart

EPITAPHS

You can count for
as long as you like,
but I'm not getting
up this time.

Former world boxing champion Jim Watt's suggestion

The defence rests.

Suggested epitaph for a lawyer

Here lies Harry Secombe
until further notice.

Harry Secombe's suggestion

Jesus Christ – is that
the time already?

Billy Connolly's suggestion

Excuse my dust.

Dorothy Parker

On my gravestone I'd like them to put, 'He didn't know what he was doing'.

Terry Wogan

———•———

I want my epitaph to be what I once read on my dry cleaning receipt: 'It distresses us to return work that is not perfect'.

Peter O'Toole

———•———

Here lies my husband – stiff at last.

Ernest Forbes' suggestion for a bitter wife

CHECKING OUT TIME

Dying is the most
embarrassing thing
that can happen to
you, because someone
else has to take care
of all your details.

Andy Warhol

Only the young die good.

Oliver Herford

—•—

Save energy. Get
cremated with a friend.

Spike Milligan

—•—

I could never bear to be buried
with people to whom I had
never been introduced.

Norman Parkinson

Dying can damage your health.
Every coffin should contain a
Government Health Warning.

Spike Milligan

—◆—

The good die young because
they see no sense in living
if you have to be good.

John Barrymore

—◆—

Old florists don't die, they just
make other arrangements.

Nigel Rees

He says it's a
marvellous business...
In 30 years he's
never had a customer
ask for a refund.

Hal Roach on an uncle's business as an undertaker

Reports of my death are
greatly exaggerated.

Mark Twain

———————

Committing suicide is the
last thing I'd ever do.

Kenny Everett

———————

If Shaw and Einstein couldn't beat
death, what chance have I got?

Mel Brooks

Last month my aunt passed away. She was cremated. We think that's what did it.

Jonathan Katz

—◦—

You live and learn, then you die and forget it all.

Nöel Coward

An undertaker is the last
man to let you down.

Danny Cummings

———

Immortality is a long shot, I admit.
But somebody has to be first.

Bill Cosby

OLD REMNANTS

As long as a woman
can look ten years
younger than her
daughter, she is
perfectly satisfied.

Oscar Wilde

A geriatric is a German
cricketer who captures three
successive wickets.

George Coote

I attribute my great age to
the simple fact that I was
born a very long time ago.

John Gielgud

There is something worse than
growing old – remaining a child.

Cesare Pavese

There are no old people
nowadays. They're either
'wonderful for their age' or dead.

Mary Pettibone Poole

━━◆━━

The older I get, the more passionate
I become about fewer things.

Brendan Kennelly

━━◆━━

Every morning when you're
93, you wake up and say to
yourself, 'What – again?'

Ben Travers

www.summersdale.com